SUBMARINES
UP CLOSE

★ **Andra Serlin Abramson** ★

STERLING

New York / London
www.sterlingpublishing.com/kids

STERLING and the distinctive Sterling logo are registered trademarks of Sterling Publishing Co., Inc.

Library of Congress Cataloging-in-Publication Data

Abramson, Andra Serlin.
  Submarines : up close / Andra Serlin Abramson.
    p. cm.
  Includes index.
  ISBN-13: 978-1-4027-4797-7
  ISBN-10: 1-4027-4797-7
  1. Submarines (Ships)--Juvenile literature. I. Title.

VM365.A37 2007
623.825'7--dc22

2006102593

10 9 8 7 6 5 4 3 2 1

Published by Sterling Publishing Co., Inc.
387 Park Avenue South, New York, NY 10016
© 2007 by Sterling Publishing Co., Inc.
Distributed in Canada by Sterling Publishing
c/o Canadian Manda Group, 165 Dufferin Street
Toronto, Ontario, Canada M6K 3H6
Distributed in the United Kingdom by GMC Distribution Services
Castle Place, 166 High Street, Lewes, East Sussex, England BN7 1XU
Distributed in Australia by Capricorn Link (Australia) Pty. Ltd.
P.O. Box 704, Windsor, NSW 2756, Australia

Cover and interior design: T. Reitzle/Oxygen-Design

Cover photo credits:
  Front and back covers (all photos), front and back flaps (background photos): Gilbert King
  Front flap: top left courtesy of MCCM Jerry McLain/DVIC; top middle courtesy of Jo1 James Pinsky, USN/DVIC;
    top right and bottom, Gilbert King
  Back flap: left © Roger Ressmeyer/CORBIS; right © Yogi, Inc./CORBIS

Printed in Thailand
All rights reserved

Sterling ISBN-13: 978-1-4027-4797-7
        ISBN-10: 1-4027-4797-7

For information about custom editions, special sales, premium and
corporate purchases, please contact Sterling Special Sales
Department at 800-805-5489 or specialsales@sterlingpub.com.

CONTENTS

· · · · · · · · · · · · · · · · · ·

This Balao class submarine can support a crew of 10 officers and 65 men for a three-month patrol. It carries 24 torpedoes, each of which holds 600 pounds of "torpex," a high explosive.

AN UNDERWATER MARVEL

WITH NEARLY THREE-QUARTERS of the Earth covered by water, it is no wonder people have been dreaming of ways to travel under the oceans for centuries. As early as 1578, inventor William Bourne wrote of "a shippe or boate that may goe under the water to the bottom, and so come up again at our pleasure."

By the American Revolution in 1775, an actual working submarine had become a reality. Submarines changed the way wars were fought, and in the nearly 250 years since the Revolutionary War, the American Navy has developed technology so advanced that most submarines are still considered "top secret."

The USS Jimmy Carter—seen here moored under a protective magnetic "silencing" cape at a naval base in Silverdale, Washington—is a nuclear-powered attack submarine of the Sea Wolf class.

Sailing on a submarine is a difficult but exciting career. More than 100 crewmembers live for months on a 300-foot-long, 30-foot-wide, three-story "building" with no windows.

There are two types of submarines. **Fast attack** submarines seek out and attack enemy ships using torpedoes and cruise missiles. **Fleet ballistic missile** subs carry long-range nuclear warheads.

Modern submarines can go anywhere in the world. This nuclear sub emerged from the ice at the Arctic Circle by using its strong metal top fin to punch a hole through the layers of ice.

DOWN THE HATCH

AIRTIGHT HATCHWAYS are the key to keeping the crew safe on a submarine. Submarines have exterior hatches that keep the water out and interior hatches that can be closed in case of an emergency. Knowing how to quickly and efficiently handle leaks is one of the most important skills a submarine crew can learn.

HOW SUBS ARE BUILT

BUILDING A NAVAL SUBMARINE is a complex, time-consuming, and expensive proposition. Each ship can cost upwards of two billion dollars and may take several years to build. The pieces of the submarine are constructed in seven different shipyards around the country, the largest of which are in Newport News, Virginia, and Groton, Connecticut. The finished pieces are then transported to a central location to be put together.

The hull, or outer shell, of the submarine is what keeps the crew safe from the surrounding water. The welded joints on the hull must be perfect.

It takes hundreds of workers with a wide range of skills—from heavy lifting to computer programming—to build a sub. Some researchers study the way fish swim to make submarines move more efficiently through the water. Other workers are responsible for welding the individual pieces of the submarine together. Still others are experts at hydraulics or engines. All these experts must work together to build one of the most technologically advanced machines ever created.

Attack submarines are usually named after cities, such as the *USS Los Angeles*. Ballistic missile submarines are named after states, like the *USS Ohio*. The newest submarines, such as the *USS Jimmy Carter* (seen on page 4), are named for famous Americans and earlier classes of submarines.

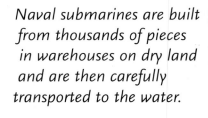

Naval submarines are built from thousands of pieces in warehouses on dry land and are then carefully transported to the water.

STEERING THE SUB

Navy submarines can dive more than 800 feet and stay submerged for several months at a time.

SUBMARINES GO UP AND DOWN in the water by using ballast tanks situated throughout the submarine. Ballast tanks work by letting seawater in and out. To dive, the sub lets in more seawater. When the tanks contain less seawater, the submarine is lighter and rises to the surface.

There are two ways for a submarine to get to the surface once it is under the water. One way is for the sub to "blow" to the surface. This can happen at any depth by blowing high-pressure air into the ballast tanks. This causes the sub to become lighter and rise. The sub can also drive to the surface by changing the position of its "wings," which are found at the front and back of the sub.

Submarines are always painted black. The color helps them hide in the water. Keeping hidden is a principal task of a submarine.

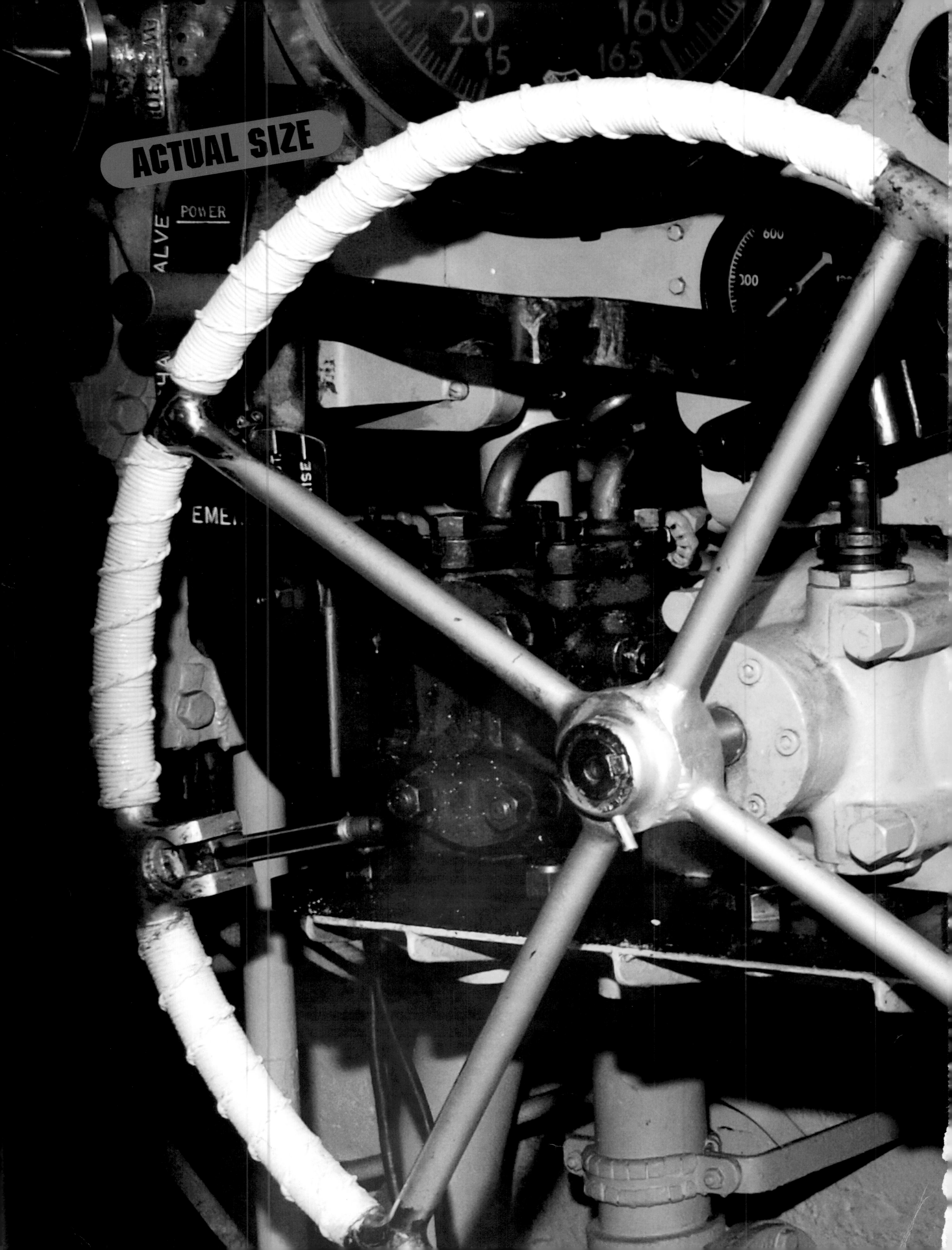
ACTUAL SIZE
20
15
160
165
POWER
ALVE
600
EMER

FIRE!

Aside from a leak, fire is another danger on a modern submarine. Most fires on a submarine are caused by faulty electrical components. Submarine crews are specially trained to put out fires, whether they occur in port or at sea. The crews carry out regular fire drills, but they do not wear fire boots or helmets. Instead, they wear special hoods called "SCBA"s, which stands for Self-Contained Breathing Apparatus. An SCBA is similar to civilian firefighting breathing devices.

Nuclear submarines have the added danger of the radioactive material they carry. The areas on the sub that carry the radioactive material are specially built to keep the crew safe. Subs also carry radiation suits for the crew to wear in case of an emergency.

The fire in the Commanding Officer's cabin on board this Canadian submarine caused a lot of damage but did not sink the sub.

ABANDON SHIP!

If an emergency forces the crew to abandon ship, they use an "escape trunk." The men put on special life preservers with hoods that provide the air needed to breathe. The hatch is then shut, and the trunk fills with water that is pressurized to sea pressure. Once this happens, the trunk's outside hatch opens, and the men are able to float to the surface.

The Navy has two rescue submarines that can navigate up to an injured submarine, attach to an escape hatch, and allow the crew to evacuate the sub.

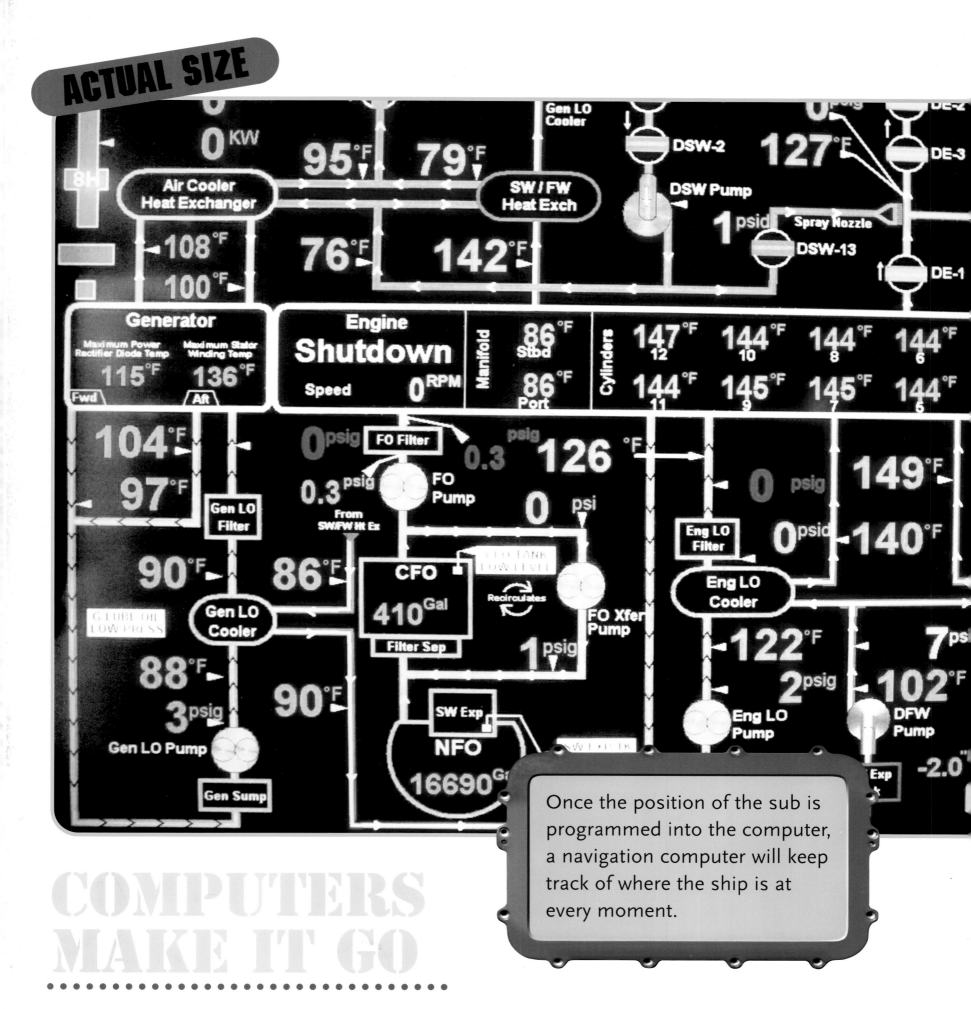

Once the position of the sub is programmed into the computer, a navigation computer will keep track of where the ship is at every moment.

COMPUTERS MAKE IT GO

SUBMARINES ARE SOME of the most technologically advanced machines ever created. Precision computers—such as the one seen above that monitors a diesel generator—assess every aspect of the submarine's environment. There are computers to check the status of the navigation system, atmosphere, sonar equipment, nuclear power, weapons, and all of the other systems.

ANGLE
INDICATOR

FULL
STROKE

HAND PUMP

3
4

1
2

1
4

ZERO
STROKE

300   1200

BOW RIG.
& WINDLASS
CLUTCH

BOW RIGGING
INDICATOR

ROCKING AND ROLLING

During normal weather conditions, a sailor on a submarine will feel much less rocking and rolling from the waves than a sailor on a boat at the surface of the water. It takes a large storm, such as a hurricane, to affect a submerged sub. Even in extremely violent weather conditions, the sub will roll only five to ten degrees. Compared to life on a surface ship, the ride is quieter and calmer.

Because the air on subs is continuously recycled and cleaned, submariners aren't used to outside smells. When the hatch is opened after months at sea, the smell of the ocean and other odors can seem very strong.

These sailors are at the helm of the USS Alabama, *a Trident missile submarine.*

MOTOR 2

VOLTS

PORT MOTORS

AMPERES

ACTUAL SIZE

Older submarines have gauges like the ones shown here. Newer submarines use digital displays and computer monitors like the one shown on the far left. The newer monitors are able to give sailors a lot more information.

To ensure the safety of the submarine and its crew, subs often have more than one computer monitoring each system. This "redundancy" creates a backup in case anything breaks down. In addition, key systems such as hatches are routinely inspected and repaired by the crew.

Nuclear-powered submarines can go about 29 miles per hour (46 kilometers per hour) underwater for an indefinite period of time.

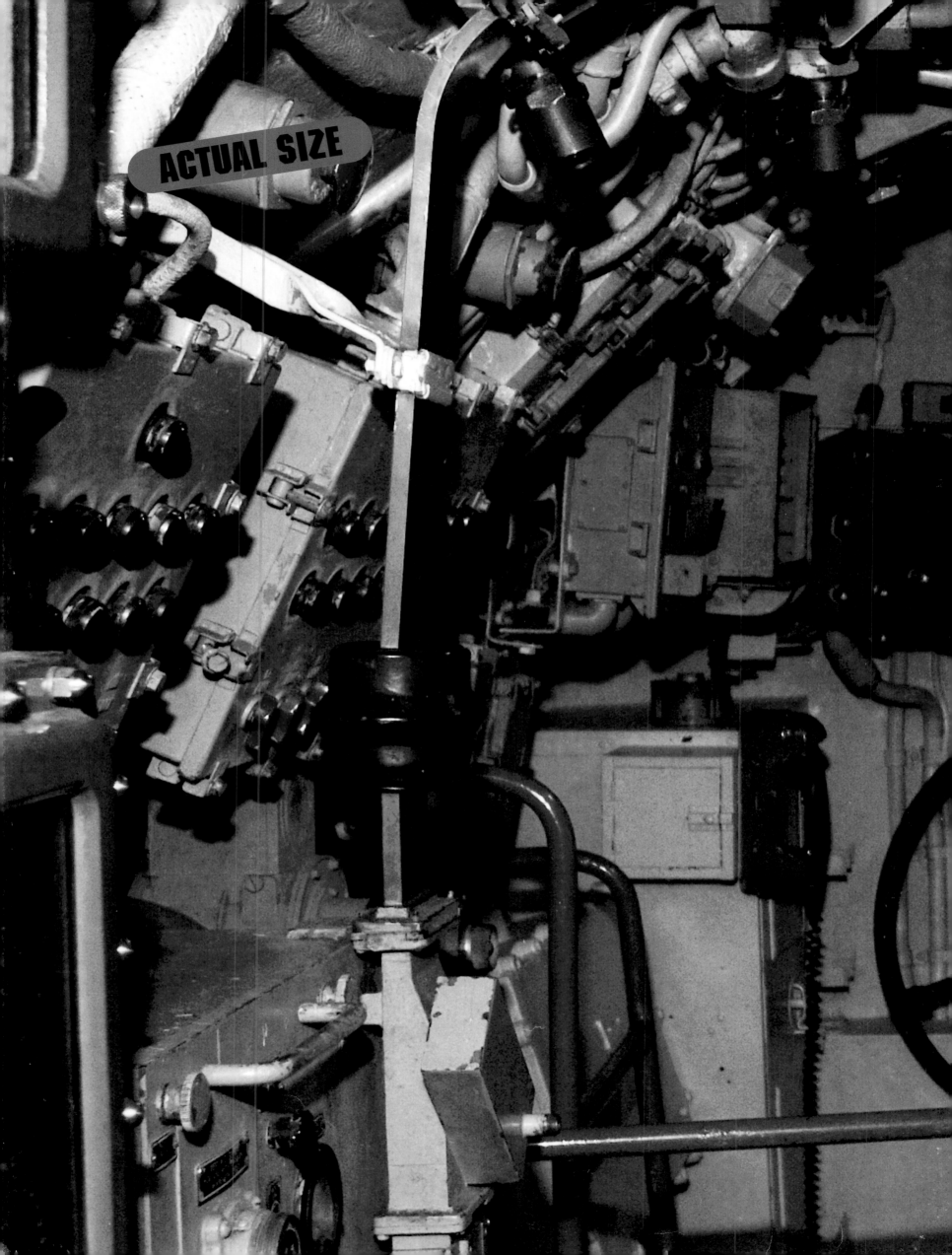
ACTUAL SIZE

SONAR: SOUND, NAVIGATION, AND RANGING

J UST AS WHALES use sound waves to find their prey, submarines use sonar to detect their targets. As a submarine cruises through the water, it creates noises that bounce off anything that is near it. A sonar computer evaluates these echoes and uses them to determine the location of the object.

ACTIVE OR PASSIVE?

Two different kinds of sonar are used to find enemy submarines and other targets. The first kind, passive sonar, just listens to the sounds around the submarine to see if anything is in the area. Passive sonar is most often used because it doesn't give away the sub's position. The second kind, active sonar, sends out a pulse of sound called a "ping." The time difference between when the ping is sent out and when the echo of the ping is heard bouncing off a nearby object helps the sonar operator measure the distance to the object.

Unfortunately, the ping can be easily detected by any submarine in the area, so using active sonar may allow the submarine to become a target instead of an attacker.

The sonar room on the USS Atlanta is lit with a blue light to make it easier for the sailors to read the monitors.

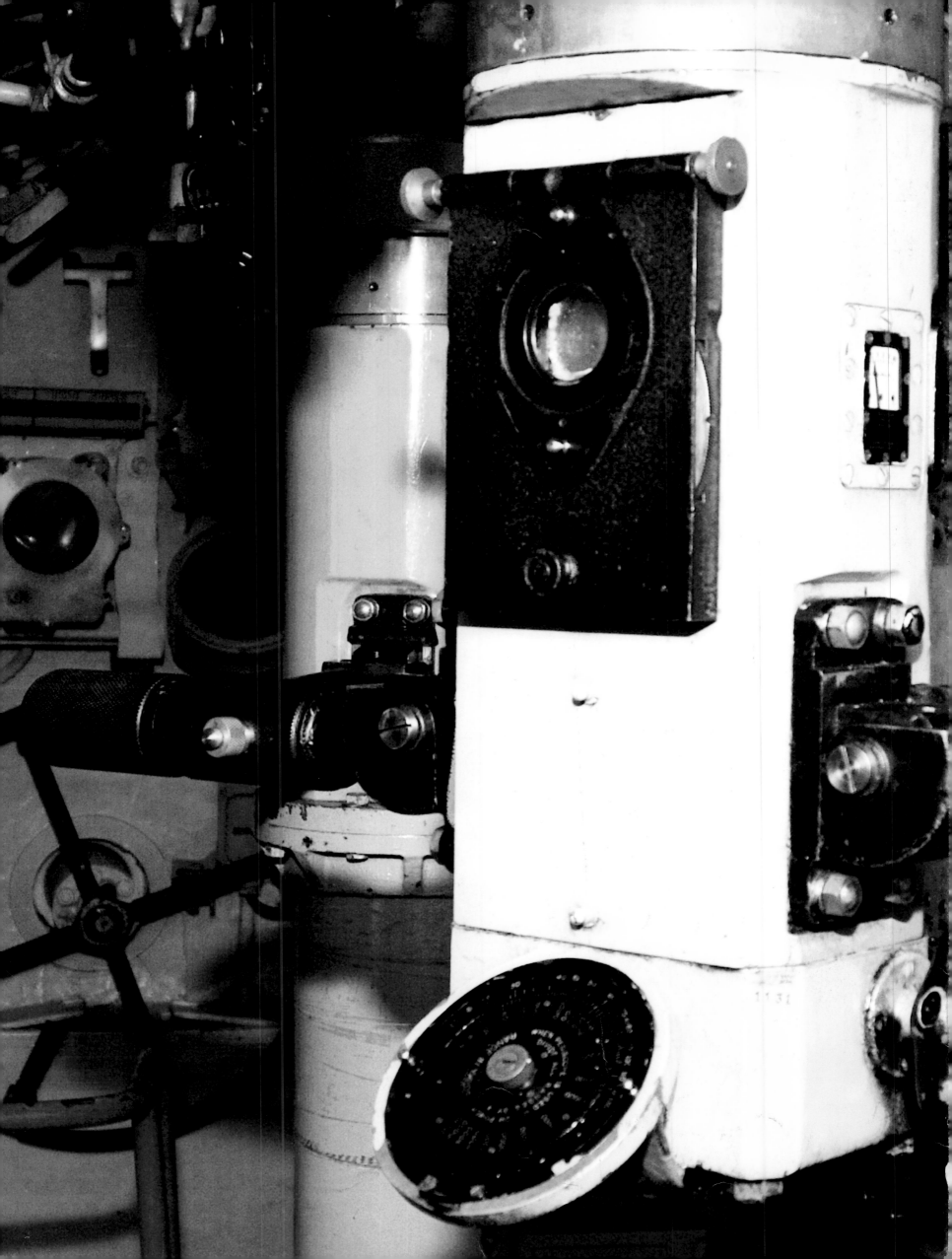

LOOK AT THAT: PERISCOPES

ONE OF THE MOST WELL-KNOWN features of a submarine is the periscope, a device that uses mirrors and other optics to see above the water outside the submarine. Before the invention of sonar, the periscope was the only way to identify a target.

ACTUAL SIZE

A search periscope allows the submariner to look for both boats on the water and aircraft in the sky. Use of the periscope can be dangerous, though. Ships and planes can use the exposed periscope to locate the submarine under the water.

A submarine needs three pieces of information to accurately attack a target: how far away it is (its "range"), the angle between the sub and its target (called the "aspect"), and the direction it is heading (known as its "bearing").

LOOK FOR YOURSELF

Looking through a real periscope is a lot like what you see in the movies. You'll see dashed lines on the eyepiece that help determine the range—the distance of a target from the sub. The periscopes on modern subs often have night vision cameras, internal antennas, and the ability to magnify the target.

COMMUNICATION WITH THE OUTSIDE WORLD

Modern submarines use satellites to communicate with the outside world. Subs can send and receive voice and non-voice communication, and they can even get e-mail. During long deployments at sea, the crew can also receive communication from home known as "family grams," a type of email that is sent through the Navy Information Operation Detachment (NIOD Groton).

During wartime, when a submarine needs to remain hidden, it may release a trailing antenna to receive news and intelligence from the outside world. A trailing antenna runs from the sub and floats on the surface of the water. It allows the sub to stay completely below water.

Sonar doesn't just pick up the sounds of other ships and subs. Sonar operators can hear whales, dolphins, and other sea creatures. They must be trained well to identify the many different sounds under the sea.

This conning tower is located directly above the submarine's control room.

REAS

CREASE

MOT. VM

SURFACE		
BELL	AHEAD	BACK
⅓	70 R.P.M.	70
⅔	140 R.P.M.	140
STD.	170 R.P.M.	
FULL		
EMERG.	100%	

BATTERY		
⅓	70 R.P.M.	70 R.P.M.
⅔	100 R.P.M.	100 R.P.M.
STD.	125 R.P.M.	125 R.P.M.
FULL	160 R.P.M.	160 R.P.M.
EMERG.	100%	100%

GIN

THE CONTROL ROOM

THE HEART OF THE SHIP is the control room. The Officer of the Deck stands his watch here, controlling all activities on board the submarine. In the control room, the ship's location is monitored, the course and depth are controlled, and all sonar contacts are tracked. The control room also functions as the attack center, where all of the ship's weapon systems are managed.

Crewmembers who drive the submarine are called the "helmsmen" and "planesmen." Their job is to keep the sub level. Like an airplane, the angle of the sub is adjusted by using a rudder and "wings" (called "diving planes") on the bow and stern. As seen in the photo below, sitting behind the helmsman and planesman is the diving officer who oversees them.

A TYPICAL DAY

Submarine crews are divided into three groups, or watch sections. Each group is on duty for 6 hours and then off duty for the next 12 hours, so a typical day on a submarine lasts 18 hours instead of the usual 24. During a regular day at sea, each watch will have about 25 crewmembers on duty at a time. However, when entering or leaving port, or when in battle conditions, every crewmember will have a watch station.

While on board a submarine, crewmembers wear a special uniform that's designed to be comfortable and reduce the amount of laundry each sailor creates. These one-piece coveralls are called "poopy suits."

During the 12 hours that a crewmember is not on watch, he can eat, sleep, attend training sessions, perform routine equipment maintenance, exercise, or just relax with a book, movie, or board game.

PROPULSION CONTROL 3W39A4
MADE FOR
BUREAU OF SHIPS
GENERAL ELECTRIC COMPANY
VOLTS 415
U.S. PAT. 1822742
1875561 2027
SERIAL NO.1   1945

CLUTCH HANDLE IN VERTICAL POSITION
FOR INDIVIDUAL TURBINA OPERATION

INCREASE   REASE   INCREA

GENERAL GE ELECTRI

MEALS UNDER THE SEA

· ·

At the beginning of a long voyage, the amount of food required to feed the crew is far greater than the available storage space. Cans of food are stored on the floors of the sub throughout the ship.

IMAGINE BEING IN A windowless house for months at a time, never going outside or seeing the sun. That's what life is like for a submarine crew. It can be a long and difficult tour of duty with tight quarters and little access to entertainment. To keep morale high, the Navy makes sure the sailors on a submarine eat well. Each sub may have as many as four chefs who are trained much like the chefs on luxury cruise ships.

The amount of food a submarine takes on its voyage is the main limitation on how long the sub can stay at sea. Subs usually carry enough food for three months, plus a little extra for emergencies. Like all spaces on a sub, the galley—or kitchen—is cramped. Deep freezers, refrigerators, coffee makers, and other equipment take up most of the space. There is only a small work space for each member of the crew assigned to the galley.

MEET IN THE MESS

The crew on a submarine eats in what's called the mess hall, where food is served 24 hours a day. The mess hall also functions as a social space where crewmembers can play games such as backgammon or cards, and also gives the crew a little bit of space to spread out and read a book or watch a movie.

Not everyone has what it takes to be a submariner. Volunteers must pass suitability tests and attend school to get specialized training. The highest honor a submariner can receive is to earn the right to wear the gold or silver dolphin emblem on his uniform. This emblem shows that the sailor is "qualified in submarines" and has had training on every system on the ship.

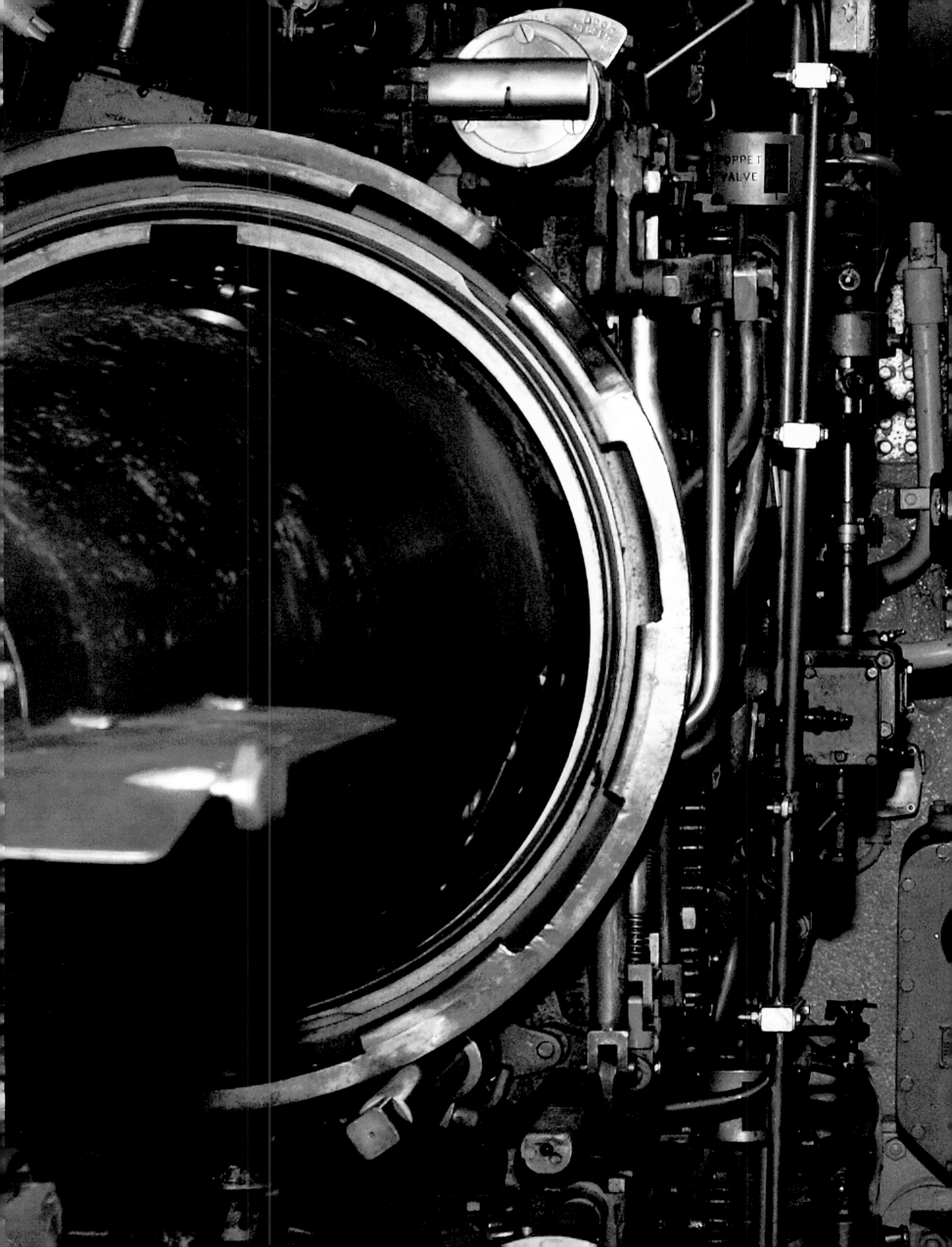

"MAN THE TORPEDOES!"

FOR A SAILOR ON A SUBMARINE, no words are more exciting or more dangerous. Torpedoes were first used on submarines during the 1870s, and by World War I, virtually every submarine carried this impressive weapon. The original torpedoes required the captain to correctly calculate the size, depth, and speed of the target in order to get a direct hit. Today's torpedoes use complex computer systems to guide the weapon where it needs to go.

To help protect the submarine in case of an attack, some subs have machine guns mounted on the deck.

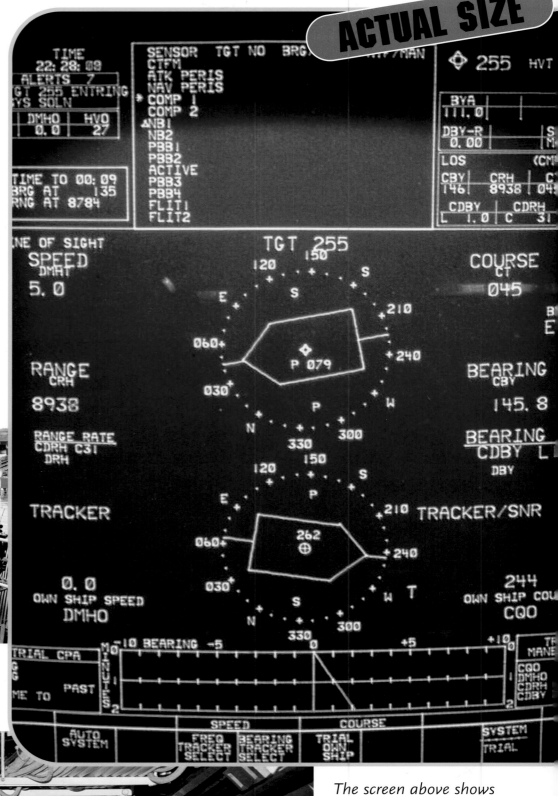

ACTUAL SIZE

The screen above shows the torpedo fire control system on the Los Angeles class submarine USS Salt Lake City.

The open torpedo tube shown at left is on the USS Hartford, a Los Angeles class nuclear-powered fast attack submarine.

MODERN WARFARE

Modern-day submarines are equipped with missiles that can launch from underwater and attack targets thousands of miles away on land or at sea. Submarines may carry two different kinds of missiles. Ballistic missiles with nuclear warheads have thankfully never been used. They are deterrents that keep other nations from using nuclear weapons against the United States. Cruise missiles are capable of striking a specific spot hundreds of miles away.

Submarines may also carry torpedoes and mines. Mines can be laid without the submarine's location being given away. These mines are hidden in the water, usually in an enemy harbor or shipping lane, and can be programmed to go off only when they detect a ship nearby. Mines can even be programmed to allow a certain number of ships to pass by before the mine detonates.

A United States Navy fleet ballistic missile submarine carries as many as 24 Trident missiles with nuclear warheads. Each missile is stored in its own separate launch tube.

Everything on a submarine is constantly cleaned and monitored. Here, a sailor is cleaning a torpedo on the USS Norfolk.

Fast attack submarines launched cruise missiles against targets during Operation Desert Storm in Iraq (1991) and against Serbia during the conflict in Kosovo (1999).

GOING TO THE HEAD

IN THE OLD DAYS, submarines carried a limited amount of fresh water and didn't have the power to recycle the water. As a result, sailors took very few showers. The one exception was the cook, who was allowed to take as many showers as he wanted in order to keep illnesses on board to a minimum.

On a submarine, fresh water is used for showers, sinks, cooking, and cleaning. Seawater is used to flush toilets, and the resulting "black water" is stored in a sanitary tank until it is pumped overboard using a special sanitary pump. Water from showers and sinks is stored separately in "gray water" tanks, which are pumped overboard using the drain pump.

WIPE DOWN SINK
AFTER EACH USE

Because there is so little room on a submarine, there is usually only one washer and one dryer on board. Laundry is done weekly by division on a rotating schedule.

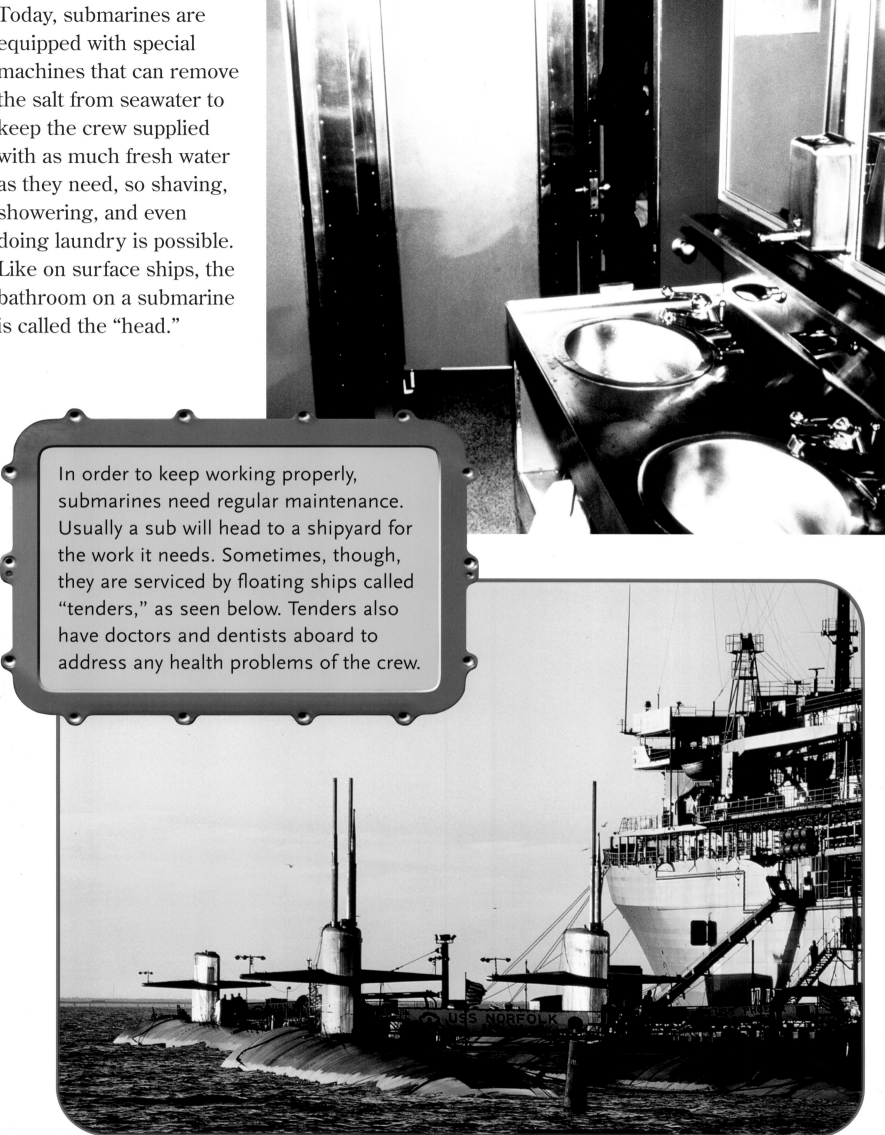

Today, submarines are equipped with special machines that can remove the salt from seawater to keep the crew supplied with as much fresh water as they need, so shaving, showering, and even doing laundry is possible. Like on surface ships, the bathroom on a submarine is called the "head."

In order to keep working properly, submarines need regular maintenance. Usually a sub will head to a shipyard for the work it needs. Sometimes, though, they are serviced by floating ships called "tenders," as seen below. Tenders also have doctors and dentists aboard to address any health problems of the crew.

BERTHING AREAS

Old-time submarines often had so little usable space that sailors slept side-by-side with the torpedoes. As you can see in the photo above, some bunks were even suspended just above weapons.

THE LIVING QUARTERS on a submarine are called "berthing areas." A berthing area has no more than 15 square feet of space for each crewman to sleep and store personal belongings. Each bunk on a modern submarine has a reading light, a ventilation duct, a curtain for privacy, and an earphone jack for the ship's on-board audio entertainment system.

Women are not currently allowed to serve as submariners in the US Navy. This is because of the limited amount of privacy and the lack of space for separate sleeping and bathroom areas.

The officers of the submarine share slightly more private quarters than the rest of the crew, with three people sharing one stateroom. Officers also have their own mess hall called the "wardroom."

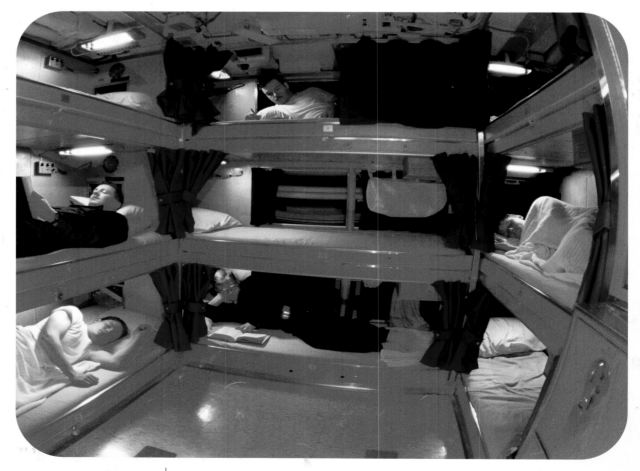

Even modern submarines allow each sailor very little personal space.

INDEX

PHOTO CREDITS